Tiger's Legendary Heroes

Kate Scott
Illustrations by Anthony J Foti
Character illustrations by Jonatronix

Contents

What makes a hero legendary?	2
Legend or Myth?	4
Standing up to bullies: Boudica	7
The trickster: Björn Ironside	9
A hero in disguise: Hua Mulan	11
How do legends grow?	12
Not all heroes are human: Warrior	13
Ordinary heroes	15
Overcoming problems: Sundiata Keita	16
Against the odds: Spartacus	19
Boldly being first: Amelia Earhart	22
A fierce foe: Geronimo	24
Unbeatable: Alexander the Great	27
Secrets of the legends	30
Glossary	31
Index	32

What makes a hero legendary?

Heroes do brave and daring things. The bravest and most daring heroes become legends – and that's what I want to be! I want people to talk about my courage, strength and amazing adventures.

I work hard at school, and I'm captain of the football team, so that's a start! But how can I turn myself from ordinary boy into **legendary** hero?

To get some tips, I'm going to look at ten heroes from history. Their stories will help me work out how to become a legend!

Who will be my top legendary hero? I've got ten heroes in mind but which one will be number one? Can you guess?

The legendary hero Hercules fighting the monster Hydra.

What is a legend?

Most legends are thought to be based on true stories. They got told over and over again until they were famous. The star of each legend is a real person – usually a strong leader with lots of courage. Some of the first legendary heroes lived in Ancient Greece and Rome.

Legendary heroes can come from anywhere in the world, at any time in history. They all share good human qualities. These are things such as courage, strength, cleverness and leadership.

Amelia Earhart
1897–1937
USA

King Arthur
5th–6th centuries AD
UK

Bjorn Ironside
9th century AD
Sweden

Boudica
around 30–60 BC
UK

Alexander the Great
356–323 BC
Ancient Greece

Warrior
1908–1941
UK

Hua Mulan
AD 581–618
China

Geronimo
1829–1909
Mexico

Spartacus
109–71 BC
Ancient Greece

Sundiata Keita
around 1210–1255
Africa

To help me decide who my number one hero is, I've awarded each hero points for their heroic qualities. See if you agree with my scores!

Hero Rating

COURAGE ?
STRENGTH ?
CLEVERNESS ?
LEADERSHIP ?
SUCCESS ?

10 Legend or myth?

Born: United Kingdom
Lived: 5th or 6th century AD

KING ARTHUR is one of the most famous legendary heroes in history but no one knows if any of the stories about him are true!

The facts?

Most **historians** agree that Arthur was probably a Welsh king. He is thought to have lived around 1500 years ago, and defended Britain against the **Saxons** in the early 6th century.

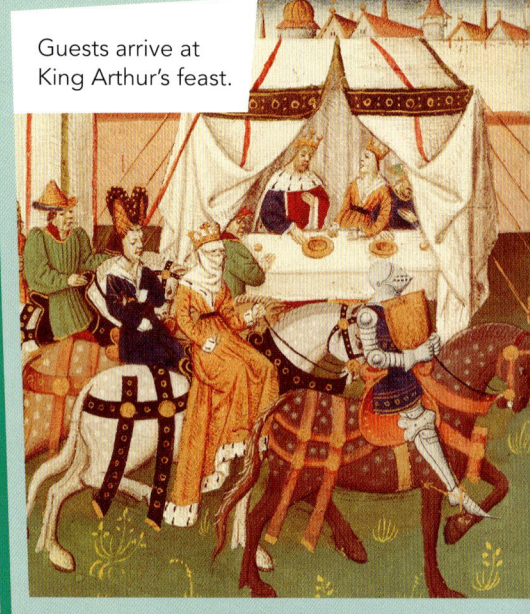

Guests arrive at King Arthur's feast.

The legend begins …

Most stories about King Arthur were written hundreds of years after he was supposed to have lived. It was after this that the legends of King Arthur became well known. The most exciting stories – like Arthur being helped by a magician called Merlin – were fiction.

These stories are called the Arthurian Legends. They have been retold in novels, poems, television programmes and films. King Arthur became famous even though he may never have existed!

The Tigerian Legends – I can picture it now!

Excalibur

King Arthur is said to have had a sword called 'Excalibur'. Two legends describe how the sword came to be his.

The Sword in the Stone

The first legend says that Merlin sent for all the lords who wanted to be king. When they arrived, they found a large marble stone with a sword trapped in it. An **inscription** on the stone said that the person who could remove the sword would be the rightful king of England. Merlin **prophesied** that Arthur could do it.

Each lord tried to pull the sword from the stone – but they couldn't move it. It was stuck fast.

Then Arthur, who was only a boy, came forward. He put his hands around the handle of the sword and pulled … and out it came!

Because the lords had all seen Arthur perform this amazing act, they were forced to support him as king even though he was just a boy.

Arthur pulling the sword from the stone.

Arthur pulling the sword from the stone.

The Lady of the Lake

The second legend says that when Arthur became king, he complained to Merlin that he had no sword. So Merlin led him to a lake and rowed him to the middle of the water.

A woman appeared and walked over the surface of the water. Merlin told Arthur that she was the Lady of the Lake and that he should ask her for a sword. An arm rose up from the water, holding a sword. The Lady of the Lake agreed Arthur could take it.

There are many different versions of each story – see how many you can find!

The stories about King Arthur are amazing. He makes my top ten, even if they're not true!

Hero Rating **40**

COURAGE	08
STRENGTH	08
CLEVERNESS	08
LEADERSHIP	08
SUCCESS	08

INSPIRED: Hundreds of books, films and TV programmes

9 Standing up to bullies

Born: South-east England
Lived: around 30–60 BC

BOUDICA was a brave queen who led an army against the mighty Roman Empire!

Boudica's story

Boudica was the queen of the Iceni people. They were an ancient British tribe. She was married to Prasutagus. When he died, Prasutagus wanted his kingdom to be shared between his daughters and the Roman Empire. Instead the Romans **seized** everything he had. When Boudica protested, the Romans whipped her in public and attacked her daughters. Boudica decided to go to war …

Boudica means 'Victoria', which comes from the Latin for 'victory'.

"I am not fighting for my kingdom and wealth now. I am fighting as an ordinary person for my lost freedom, my bruised body, and my outraged daughters."

Boudica

Romans out!

Boudica put together an army of men, women and children. Everyone wanted to force the Romans out. Her army destroyed three cities under Roman control: Colchester, London and St Albans. They killed many Romans and destroyed anything that had been built by them.

The big battle

Boudica led 200 000 people against the Romans but the Roman soldiers were very organized and well trained for battle. They defeated Boudica with a much smaller army. The Roman Empire was again safe.

Creating a legend

As stories are passed on, people often add details. Sometimes they want to make a legend even more exciting. Sometimes they are not sure what really happened, so they make it up. There are different versions of what happened to Boudica after her army was defeated. Some say she killed herself with poison while others say she fell ill and died.

Boudica leading her army.

Although she didn't win in the end, Boudica was incredibly brave.

Hero Rating 41

COURAGE	09
STRENGTH	08
CLEVERNESS	07
LEADERSHIP	09
SUCCESS	08

INSPIRED: Film and TV series

8 The trickster

Born: Sweden
Lived: 9th century AD

Bravery can make a hero legendary, but so can brains! BJÖRN IRONSIDE was a Viking king who became famous for his cunning raids.

The trick

Björn wanted to attack Luna, a city in Italy. However, he was unable to get past the city walls. Björn sent a messenger into the town to say that Björn had died, and that he had always wanted to be buried in Luna. Björn climbed into a coffin. A small group of his followers took him through the gates. Once he was in Luna, Björn leaped out of his coffin, fought his way to the gates, and let his army in!

Björn Ironside was brave *and* clever.

I'm sure I could think up a trick as clever as that!

Sound familiar?

There is a similar story of cunning and trickery in Greek legend, about a wooden horse built to capture the city of Troy.

The Trojan Horse, from Warner Bros. Pictures' film *Troy*.

The Trojan War between the Ancient Greeks and the people of Troy lasted ten years. During that time the Greeks had been unable to battle past Troy's strong defences. The Greeks decided to build an enormous wooden horse. They hid some soldiers inside it. As the Greek army pretended to sail away, the Trojans pulled the horse inside the city gates. When night fell, the soldiers hidden in the horse crept out and let the rest of the Greek army into the city. The Greeks destroyed Troy and won the war.

Dragon ships ahoy!

Björn Ironside travelled in longships, also known as 'dragon ships', when he led the Vikings on their raids. The low sides of the dragon ships made it easier to jump out and start fighting (and jump back in to make a quick escape!).

Vikings must have been really tough – they rowed those ships for thousands of miles!

Hero Rating **42**

COURAGE	08
STRENGTH	08
CLEVERNESS	09
LEADERSHIP	09
SUCCESS	08

INSPIRED: TV series

7 A hero in disguise

Born: Northern China
Lived: 581–618 AD

HUA MULAN was a girl who dressed up as her father to become a hero!

Undiscovered

When Hua Mulan's father was called up into the army, she knew he was too old and wouldn't survive. So Hua Mulan put on her father's clothes and took his place! She spent twelve years fighting in the army. No one realized she wasn't a man.

Hua Mulan was a brave fighter, but at the end of her army service she refused to accept any reward. Instead, she returned to her village and lived quietly with her family.

A traditional Chinese painting of Hua Mulan.

Hua Mulan's story was originally described in a Chinese poem called the *Ballad of Mulan* (木蘭辭). It first appeared in the 6th century. Over time, it has become one of the most popular Chinese legends.

Heroes don't always expect a reward!

Hero Rating: 43

COURAGE	10
STRENGTH	09
CLEVERNESS	09
LEADERSHIP	06
SUCCESS	09

INSPIRED: More than 15 films and TV programmes

How do legends grow?

Everyone loves a good story – particularly if it involves exciting events. When someone hears a terrific tale, they tell it to someone else, and that person passes it on to someone else. When artists and writers hear the story, they may be **inspired** to paint a picture, write a book or a poem, **dramatize** it by writing a play or making a film. Eventually, the original story becomes a mix of truth and fiction.

So this is how stories about legendary heroes change over time!

6 Not all heroes are human

Born: Isle of Wight, UK
Lived: 1908–1941

Can an animal be a legendary hero? Of course!

WARRIOR was a horse who belonged to General Jack Seely in World War I. He showed enormous courage in frightening, noisy battles. Once, he missed getting shot by just a few centimetres.

22nd August 1914

Today we fought at the Battle of Mons. The noise of the guns was so loud I thought my ears would explode!

I was crouched down low to the ground, my feet sinking into the mud, when I saw him: our General Jack Seely riding on his horse, Warrior. Now I know why they call him Warrior! The guns were booming but that horse didn't even blink – he just kept on carrying his General forward into the battle.

Seeing that horse be so brave made me push forward again. If that horse could be a hero, I could try, too …

Jack Seely riding Warrior in 1934.

Safe return

Hundreds of thousands of horses died in battle during World War I. Warrior's story helped make people aware of their **plight**. In 1919, Winston Churchill, who was the British Secretary of State for War, made sure the horses returned home from France safely.

Horses in battle during World War I.

So Warrior's heroism helped other horses, too …

The Dickin Medal

The PDSA (People's Dispensary for Sick Animals) Dickin Medal was created in 1943. It is given to animals that have performed courageous actions in war. The first award was given to three messenger pigeons that helped rescue people from an aeroplane in World War II. Since then, the medal has been awarded to 32 pigeons, 18 dogs, three horses and one cat!

One story leads to another

Author Michael Morpurgo's book *War Horse*, about a horse's experience during World War I, was turned into a play and a film.

Hero Rating 44

COURAGE	10
STRENGTH	10
CLEVERNESS	09
LEADERSHIP	06
SUCCESS	09

INSPIRED: Book, film and stage play

Ordinary heroes

What would you do if you saw someone in danger? Many ordinary people behave like heroes when they see people who need help.

In the UK, awards called the George Cross and the George Medal are given to **civilians** who have acted bravely in extreme danger. Patrick King, an air-raid warden during World War II, was the first person to receive the George Medal. He was given the award in 1940 for rescuing a blind woman trapped in the wreckage of her bombed house. Daniel John Collins received the medal in 1941 when he rescued a woman and two children from their bombed home.

King George set up the George Cross and the George Medal in 1940 – and gave them his name!

Patrick King and Daniel John Collins faced scenes like this.

I hope I'd be as brave as that in extreme danger!

5 Overcoming problems

Born: Mali, West Africa
Lived: around 1210-1255

SUNDIATA KEITA, also known as the Lion King of Mali, rescued his people from a cruel leader and started a new empire, but first he had to overcome many problems …

Sundiata, the Lion King of Mali

The trials of the Lion King

When Sundiata was born, he was unable to use his legs. He was determined to overcome his disability and legend says that he taught himself to walk – but this was not the end of his troubles. When his father the king died, Sundiata's half-brother drove him and his mother into **exile** for many years. They finally found a home with the King of Mema, who admired Sundiata's courage and determination.

Prophecies and predictions

Before Sundiata was born, it was predicted that he would be a great leader one day. Because of this prophecy, messengers from his homeland, Mali, were sent to find Sundiata and bring him back. The King of Mema gave Sundiata an army to return with. Sundiata rescued his people from the cruel leadership of his half-brother and became the first Emperor of the Mali Empire.

There were prophecies about King Arthur, Sundiata and my number one hero, too. Perhaps I need someone to predict that I will become a great hero!

A gold dust spoon was used to weigh gold dust.

Gold!

Sundiata's empire became very rich by trading gold, salt and copper. By the beginning of the 14th century, almost half the world's gold came from the Mali Empire. People traded in gold dust, while solid gold was kept in the **treasury** (like a bank account).

Salt was also very valuable because it was so rare – it was sometimes considered more valuable than gold!

The hardships of heroes

Heroes often become legendary for the way they face and overcome problems. Boudica was whipped, Spartacus (see page 19) was forced to be a gladiator, and Sundiata taught himself to walk and survived exile.

The Sankarani River, where some historians think Sundiata drowned.

Fact or fiction?

- Most legends mix facts, fiction and details that are somewhere in-between. Historians study **sources** to try and work out the truth.

- Using the evidence they have about Sundiata's life, most historians agree that Sundiata died around 1255.

- Did Sundiata drown, was he shot with an arrow or was he **assassinated**? Most historians think he drowned in Mali's Sankarani River, where there is a **shrine** in his name.

Hero Rating 45

COURAGE	10
STRENGTH	07
CLEVERNESS	09
LEADERSHIP	10
SUCCESS	09

INSPIRED: Books, poems and songs

Sundiata's body might not have been very strong but his mind was!

4 Against the odds

Born: Thrace, Ancient Greece
Lived: 109–71 BC

SPARTACUS was the most famous gladiator who ever lived. Together with a small number of other gladiators, he fought an army of Romans – and won!

From slave to gladiator

Spartacus was a **slave**, one of many captured by the Romans across the Roman Empire. He, along with other slaves, was forced to fight as a gladiator. In Ancient Rome, gladiators were trained to fight – often to the death. People watched these fights the way we watch TV and films today. When gladiators weren't fighting, they were kept locked up in 'Gladiator School'.

A sculpture of Spartacus.

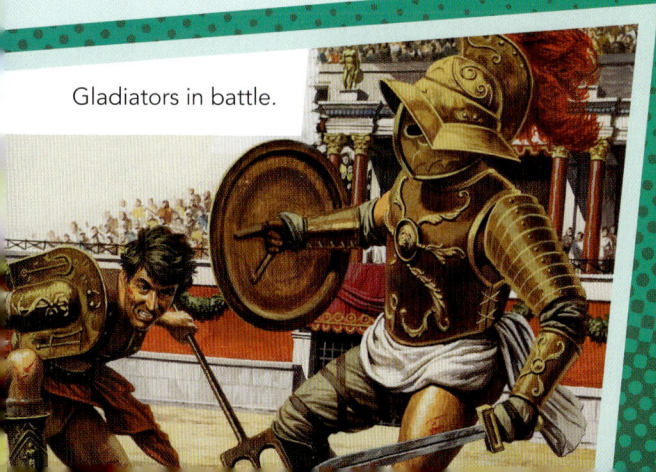

Gladiators in battle.

> I don't fancy being locked up in any kind of school!

The great escape

Spartacus escaped with a small group of gladiators. They stole weapons to defend themselves from the Romans and camped on Mount Vesuvius. Three thousand Roman soldiers were sent to capture them. With Spartacus as leader, the tiny army attacked the Roman soldiers and won.

Then Rome sent thousands more soldiers ... and Spartacus's army of slaves-turned-gladiators won that battle, too! Tens of thousands more slaves escaped to join Spartacus when they heard about his success. Historians think his army grew to 100 000 men!

Spartacus leading the slaves in revolt.

A mysterious end

Spartacus and his army were eventually defeated but many of the slaves escaped to the Italian mountains. No one knows what happened to Spartacus. His body was never found.

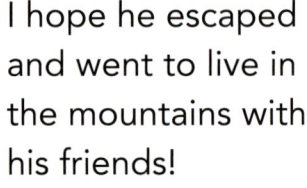

I hope he escaped and went to live in the mountains with his friends!

Fighting injustice

Spartacus stood up to the Roman Empire and fought against the cruel treatment of slaves. Legendary heroes are often famous for fighting **injustice** – especially when they stand up to people more powerful than themselves.

Spartacus inspired thousands of slaves when he was alive. His story still inspires writers, film-makers and many other people today. There are even football clubs named after him!

A battle scene from the classic film *Spartacus*, made in 1960

Spartacus's bravery and leadership made him world-famous – I'd love to have a football club named after me!

Dear Mother,

We are once more free men! Spartacus has shown so much courage. He inspires us all. At the beginning, there was only a small group of us but now we have defeated thousands of Roman soldiers!

The name of Spartacus will live on long after us – I have so many stories about him. I hope to come home one day and tell you all of them.

Your loving son,

Caesaris

Hero Rating: 46

COURAGE	10
STRENGTH	10
CLEVERNESS	09
LEADERSHIP	10
SUCCESS	07

INSPIRED: Books, films, TV series, cartoons and comic books

3 Boldly being first

Born: Kansas, USA
Lived: 24th July 1897 – 2nd July 1937

Flying firsts!

- **1922:** Breaks women's altitude record after rising to 14 000 feet
- **1928:** First woman to fly across the Atlantic
- **1930:** Sets speed record of 181.18 mph
- **1931:** Sets women's **autogiro** altitude record with 18 415 feet
- **1932:** First woman to fly solo across the Atlantic
- **1932:** First woman to fly solo non-stop across the USA coast-to-coast
- **1935:** First person to fly solo across the Pacific between Honolulu in Hawaii and California
- **1935:** First person to fly solo from Los Angeles to Mexico City
- **1935:** First person to fly solo non-stop from Mexico City to Newark
- **1937:** First person to fly from the Red Sea to India

AMELIA EARHART liked to be first – she set or broke more than ten flying records!

Flying ahead

In 1928, Earhart was the first woman to fly across the Atlantic Ocean. Along with two male co-pilots, she flew from Newfoundland in Canada to Burry Port in Wales. It took them nearly 21 hours. This flight wasn't enough for Amelia, though. She was now determined to fly across the Atlantic on her own and, in 1932, she did!

Route taken on Amelia Earhart's final flight.

Earhart goes missing during world flight

3rd July 1937

Amelia Earhart disappeared yesterday, during her attempt to be the first person to fly around the world.

Her plane was last heard from while crossing the Pacific Ocean. It is thought that she and her **navigator**, Fred Noonan, went off course on their way to refuel at Howland Island.

Amelia Earhart with her plane

Hero Rating: 47

- COURAGE 10
- STRENGTH 10
- CLEVERNESS 10
- LEADERSHIP 07
- SUCCESS 10

INSPIRED: Books, films and comic books

People still don't know what happened to Amelia Earhart. Mystery can help make a hero legendary, too!

2 A fierce foe

Born: No-Doyohn Canyon, Mexico
Lived: 1829–1909

GERONIMO was leader of the Native American Bedonkohe Apache tribe in New Mexico. He was one of the fiercest fighters in history!

The making of a warrior

Geronimo was away from home when Mexican soldiers attacked his **settlement**. He returned to find his mother, wife and children had been killed.

From that moment, Geronimo dedicated himself to revenge, and fighting for his people's right not to be forced off their land by white settlers. He rose up and lead his tribe to defend their land.

Geronimo was born in No-Doyohn Canyon, Mexico.

Geronimo vowed to protect his homeland for his tribe.

"I was born on the prairies where the wind blew free and there was nothing to break the light of the sun. I was born where there were no **enclosures**."

"I was no chief and never had been, but because I had been more deeply wronged than others, this honor was conferred upon me, and I **resolved** to prove worthy of the trust."

Geronimo

Geronimo (on the right) with a small group of followers in 1886.

Geronimo as an old man.

Skeleton Canyon

Though he fought hard and escaped capture many times, Geronimo was finally defeated on 4th September 1886 at Skeleton Canyon, Arizona. He was then forced to live on a **reservation** in Oklahoma, far from his home.

In his old age, Geronimo became famous. He sold photographs of himself and even took part in important parades. He was never allowed to go back to the land where he had been born.

Geronimo's best quality is that he never wanted to give up.

The grave of Geronimo in Fort Sill, Oklahoma, USA.

Did you know?

- Geronimo was said to be bulletproof. This was definitely not true but he wasn't scared of bullets!

- Geronimo's skull went missing after he died. We know his bones were dug up and even today no one is sure where they are …

- Geronimo was not his real name. When he was born, he was called Goyahkla (said to mean 'One Who Yawns'). There are lots of theories about how he came to be known as 'Geronimo' but no one is sure of the answer.

Hero Rating 48

COURAGE	10
STRENGTH	10
CLEVERNESS	10
LEADERSHIP	10
SUCCESS	08

INSPIRED: Books, films and a catch-phrase!

Fierce Geronimo wasn't scared of anything! Today, people sometimes shout 'Geronimo' when doing something dangerous, to show they have no fear.

1 Unbeatable

Born: Pella, Ancient Greece
Lived: 356–323 BC

It's time to announce my top legendary hero! He may have lived more than 2000 years ago, but he was so clever that people still use his ideas today!

Alexander the Great's Empire over 2000 years ago.

ALEXANDER THE GREAT was the most successful military leader in the history of Ancient Greece. He was never beaten in battle even though he spent his whole life waging war. He became a soldier when he was just 18 years old and was soon in charge of his own army.

The empire maker

Alexander's brilliant battle skills helped him create and rule a vast empire – it covered around five million square kilometres! He **founded** more than 70 cities and named 20 after himself, including Alexandria in Egypt.

Battle skills

One of Alexander's war-winning tricks was called the *phalanx* (Greek for 'finger'). This was a way of grouping soldiers in long, tightly packed lines. The soldiers would carry shields and spears. Using these the phalanx would break through the ranks of enemy soldiers. Alexander used the phalanx more successfully than any previous general had done before. This was because he directed the soldiers carefully and trained them to move quickly.

A great leader

Alexander trained his soldiers well and led them so bravely that in almost 13 years of constant fighting, they only refused to follow him once!

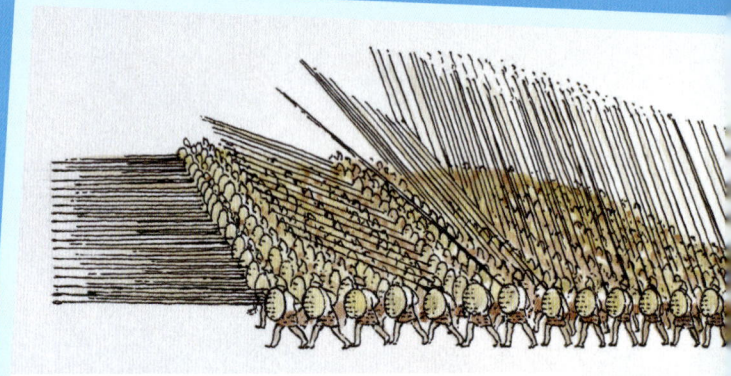

Tightly packed lines of soldiers form the phalanx

Alexander the Great was never defeated!

Fact or fiction?

Alexander died when he was just 33. No one knows why he died so young. Some people think he was poisoned but it is more likely that he died of **typhoid fever** or **malaria**.

Alexander was buried in Egypt, but the rulers who came after him moved his body more than once. There are lots of stories about where his tomb might be – and whether he is still in it!

A sculpture of Alexander the Great.

A true legend!

Alexander was brave, strong and very clever. People were loyal to him because they knew that he would never ask them to do anything he wouldn't do himself. He had countless victories and his battle **tactics** are still studied today!

Hero Rating 50
- COURAGE 10
- STRENGTH 10
- CLEVERNESS 10
- LEADERSHIP 10
- SUCCESS 10

INSPIRED: Books, films, TV programmes, songs and computer games

The thing I like most about Alexander the Great is his attitude – he thought anything was possible!

Secrets of the legends

Many legendary heroes are known for bravery in battle. Should a modern legend be defined in the same way? Bravery can be shown in many ways – sometimes the bravest thing to do is not to fight. Modern day legends, such as Nelson Mandela, fought injustice with words rather than war.

Did you spot the link between all my heroes? They never gave up! In the words of my number one hero Alexander the Great: "There is nothing impossible to him who will try." If I keep working hard, people might one day tell stories about me!

Can you think of modern-day heroes who might become legendary? They may be people who work against injustice, people who raise money for charity, or people who try to make the world more peaceful. Do you think you might have what it takes to become a legend?

Nelson Mandela spent 27 years in prison in South Africa before ruling as President from 1994 until 1999.

Glossary

assassinate	to murder someone to stop them having power
autogiro	a small plane with a rotor
civilian	someone who is an ordinary citizen and not in the army
dramatize	to write a play or make a film about something
enclosure	a fenced-off area
exile	a period when you are forced to live away from your country
found	to start an organization, city or society
historian	someone who studies or is an expert in history
injustice	something that is unfair or wrong
inscription	a set of words written or carved on something
inspire	to give people ideas or excite them to do something
legendary	very famous; described in legends
malaria	a fever passed from person to person by mosquitoes
navigator	a person who makes sure that an aircraft is going in the right direction
plight	difficulty or trouble
prophesy	say that something will happen in the future. The thing prophesied is a **prophecy**.
raid	a sudden attack
reservation	an area that is protected or controlled
resolve	to make your mind up to do something
Saxons	a group of people who settled in southern England in the 5th to 6th centuries
seize	to grab or take something
settlement	a group of people and their homes
shrine	a sacred place, or a place set up in memory of someone
slave	a person who is owned by someone else and has to work or fight for them without being paid
source	a place, person or thing which something comes from or which gives information about something
tactics	plans or methods
treasury	a place where treasure is stored
typhoid	a fever caught by drinking dirty water

Index

aeroplane	14, 23
animals	14
army	7–9, 10–11, 17, 19, 20, 27
battle	8, 10, 13, 14, 20–21, 27, 28–29
Dickin Medal	14
dragon–ships	10
Excalibur	4–5
George Medal	15
gladiator	18–20
heroes	2–4, 9, 11, 12–13, 15, 17–18, 21, 30
history	2–4, 24, 27
Lady of the Lake	6
leader	3, 16–17, 20, 24, 27, 28, 30
legends	2–5, 11, 12, 18, 30
Merlin	4–6
Mount Vesuvius	20
Romans	7–8, 19–20
slave	19–21
Troy	10
vikings	9, 10
Warrior	13, 14